The Strangest Secret to Winning Championships

J. Scott Warner

Copyright © 2012 by J. Scott Warner

All rights reserved. This book or any portion thereof may not be reproduced or used in any manner whatsoever without the express written permission of the publisher except for the use of brief quotations in a book review.

Printed in the United States of America

First Printing, 2012

ISBN 978-0615664163

A.N.T. Publishing House
www.ANTPublishingHouse.com

Dedication

This book is the culmination of thousands of hours of hard work, research and the loyal support of many people who supported my dreams of helping others reach their highest levels of achievement, win multiple championships and cement their legacy. I sincerely thank Earl Nightingale for his inspiration in this effort.

This book is also dedicated to all of my clients and colleagues who have worked with me and my team to get on their path to sports mastery and to win championships. I have been privileged to work with some of the brightest minds today and I truly thank and appreciate each one.

And finally, to all of you who are in doubt or wondering if you really "can" achieve your goals. If many others and I can do this, so can you! I look forward to helping you, not only leave your legacy but, live it today!

Testimonials

The following are just a few of the many, many people who have been impacted by the system you will discover within **"The Strangest Secret to Winning Championships"**.

"I've played pro basketball overseas and in the U.S., and I've trained with J. Scott and I personally witnessed how to apply sports mastery principles. Wow! This guy will have you on top of your game in no time. My blueprint was unlike anything I had ever seen before! If you're ready to win it all, call J. Scott today!"

M. Harrell……….............……...FIBA, PBA & All-Star Navy Team

"J. Scott's ideas and concepts are second to none! This is a powerhouse of tips, tactics and approaches for mastering your sport that simply works. A fantastic book!"

C. Nelson……................…….…San Diego Chargers, Seattle Seahawks, Boise St.

"J. Scott removes all the barriers to becoming a master in your sport. With his custom step by step blueprint, anyone can learn to master their sport and reach their highest levels of performance."

M. Coleman…......…………...……Red Sox, Yankees, Devil Rays, Reds & Alabama Crimson Tide (football)

"What J. Scott teaches about Sports Mastery is not taught in any college, university or pro facility I've seen. I'm really impressed!"

K. Robinson…........………………………….Baltimore Ravens

"**The Strangest Secret to Winning Championships** is a smash hit! Anyone who's ever wanted to win it all will definitely benefit from the cutting edge knowledge and practical wisdom in this book! Go get it, now."

J. Campbell…….......…………......…………AFL and L.A. Rams

"I've had many pro coaches and trainers and I've never seen anything that even comes close to this! A must read for any athlete that wants to win big!"

D. Jones……................……………N.Y. Knicks, Boston Celtics

"Playing on a team with J. Scott was quite an experience. He not only led us to 3 out of 5 championships as a player, when he missed one game with an ankle sprain he coached us and when I cramped up he helped stretch me out too! This guy does it all!"

E. Reid…………………………………Vanderbilt Basketball

"The great thing about J. Scott's system is that it is a complete system. Pretty much every other coach or trainer I've had only told me about "parts" of the game, but J. Scott gave me an entire system for me to reach my highest levels of achievement."

D. Walker……….................……San Francisco State Basketball

"Anybody who wants to start winning and start winning consistently NEEDS to call J. Scott! I use his principles in my coaching every day. There's nothing out there that comes close to what this guy will do for you!"

C. Landrum……...Player/Coach College of Marin Football

Table of Contents

Chapter 1 The Strangest Secret to Winning Championships Revealed..............................1

Chapter 2 Discover the Proven System for You to Master your Sport, Win championships, and be Etched into History as a Champion-In half the time!..20

Chapter 3 Right and Wrong Training Methods – Little Pointers that Will Have You Holding Up Your Trophy this Year!...................38

Chapter 4 Your Pre-Mastery Warm Up – How to Prepare Yourself to Quickly Absorb a New Revolutionary System for Winning it All When It Matters most.......................54

Chapter 5 How to Create the Mindset of a Muhammad Ali, Michael Jordan and Bruce Lee all in one!........................61

Chapter 6	Discover the Secret Foundation to Maximize your Full Athletic Potential – Save Months of Time and Energy Wasted on Peak Performance Training...................74
Chapter 7	The Nuts 'n Bolts that Will Take You from a Top Athlete to a Master in Your Sport! Unleash the Beast and Make Your Competition Run for Cover When You Enter the Arena..86
Chapter 8	R-E-S-P-E-C-T, just a little bit. Feels Pretty Good to Be a Champion, huh?.....................96
Chapter 9	How to Win Multiple Championships and Cement a Legacy that will Etch You into Sports History as a True Champion........................110

Chapter ①

The

Strangest Secret

To

Winning Championships

Revealed

Questions every athlete and coach needs to ask:

How can you stop frustrating losses even after you've tried everything?

What can you do to consistently win big and when it counts the most?

Is there a way to silence the critics that say you always choke in the big games?

How come you did everything you could, prepared for months and months and came up short when it mattered most?

Good news is, it's not entirely your fault.

One reason that many athletes are not getting the results they want and are not winning the championships they feel they deserve to win, is partly due to the thinking that has been taught, probably since the beginning of their athletic career.

It may seem ironic but, in researching and studying many of the legends in sports history, it's clearly evident that most of the true champions' main personal goals were for maximum achievement in their sport, not the actual championship.

Vince Lombardi, Championship NFL football coach and icon once stated, *"The quality of a person's life is in direct proportion to their commitment to excellence, regardless of their chosen field."*

Legendary Basketball Coach John Wooden stated, *"Success is peace of mind which is a direct result of self-satisfaction in knowing you made the effort to become the best of which you are capable."*

Even Lorena Ochoa, the first Mexican-born player to win on the L.P.G.A. Tour, stated after her victory at St. Andrews in 2007, *"I didn't struggle doubting or spending time debating...... It was clear to me that I wanted to be the best."*

> *"For me, it was to be the best athlete that I could possibly be and that also happened to be the fastest man in the history of sprinting. And I pursued the goal, not of being the fastest man, but of being the best I could possibly be."* – Michael Johnson (Olympic Record Holder and 18 Time Gold Medalist)

Once these champions' were on a quest for the highest levels of achievement, the actual winning of the championship was simply a side benefit. So, what is the secret to consistently winning championships and attaining the highest levels of athletic achievement possible? The strangest secret to winning championships lies in the very essence of what is now called, **sports mastery.**

What is Sports Mastery?

Have you ever been in a big game or event and had full control over the outcome? If you had full control, would it have turned out differently for you?

Throughout history, athletes for many years all strive to reach the highest level of achievement possible and although, called by many names, the relatively new term "Sports

Mastery" refers to the art and philosophy of mastering your sport so as to reach the highest levels of personal athletic achievement. An athlete on the path to sports mastery will be able to fully maximize his/her own athletic potential and then be able to synergistically apply it to a specific sport or event.

Although, elusive and rarely ever thought of in terms of sports, evidence of mastery is clear still today. George Leonard, American writer and renowned educator on human potential, alludes to the fact that mastery *"can instantly be recognized, yet resists definition."*

Throughout Olympic Sports history, the Soviet Union's sports program had always been on the cutting edge of athletic performance. One example of this is shown during the 1984 Summer Olympic Games that were held in Los Angeles. Due to various political reasons, the USSR and its Eastern Bloc allies all boycotted the games. Without their biggest competitors present, the American athletes captured 174 total medals. In response, the USSR and the other boycotting countries staged the 1984 Friendship Games in Moscow a few weeks later.

The results are as follows:

In track and field, of the forty-one (41) gold medals in Los Angeles, twenty-eight (28) of those final results were surpassed at the Friendship Games. In addition, in the swimming competition, five (5) world records and a total of forty (40) swimmers exceeded the time of their American competitors (74).

The difference was their superior method of training and one reason why their sports science program was so highly advanced and competitive was because it was based around their "P.A.S.M." system, (Process of Achieving Sports Mastery).

Renowned pioneers on super performance, Dr. Yuri Verkhoshansky and Dr. Mel Siff, in their new expanded version of the book "Supertraining", makes it clear that thinking in terms of sports mastery should be the foundational basis in the training of all athletes. It is clearly evident that sports mastery should be at the forefront of any serious athletes' mind.

Mastery of your sport is the highest level of achievement and thus, will produce the highest level of results. Legendary martial artist and philosopher, Bruce Lee, once stated that true mastery comes when an individual can truly and fully express himself through his discipline or art.

We don't mean being showy or haughty; but one that when the time calls for it, can express oneself through their play.

When we think about the philosophy of sport itself, we may only consider the obvious, which is to win the game or event. However, when we delve deeper, we see that the true nature of competitive sport is to find out which athlete can best express him or herself. The athletes that can best express themselves seem to, more often than not, emerge victorious.

A seemingly odd characteristic research shows is that the athlete who knows himself the best, usually can figure ways to make himself "beat" his opponent. He/she is able to spot and exploit weaknesses better and faster and perform better during critical moments while being able to hide their own weaknesses well. Of course, once you reach your sports mastery levels, your weaknesses will greatly lessen until you have none left.

Regarding expression, it can be said that the purpose of mastering a sport is to be able to fully express one's self in the given sport. If your intention is to win the championship, and you're a master in your sport, you will no doubt be able to express your desire to win it all and actually do it.

Sports Mastery is the culmination of an athletes' potential being fully realized, intertwined with expert level knowledge of his/her sport naturally fused together by internal cosmological synthesis; then implemented and exercised for actual application. Once any level of mastery is achieved, constant practice and implementation must be continued, as sports mastery is always evolving as the athlete evolves. There is an inner sports master in all of us; you just need a system that will get you back in touch with your true self.

Learning and implementing sports mastery principles is the most efficient way for the top pro athletes to truly actualize their maximum potential and relate it to their sport for their own immediate use. Sports mastery is achieved when the athlete has actualized the physical and mental aspects then synergistically tied in their expert knowledge into their sport through implementation and progression.

Each athlete's level of mastery will vary as each athlete's own innate desires and abilities vary. Every athlete is different and once mastery is achieved and true expression is realized, we will then be witness to the true beauty of sport. We will then see true art being expressed through masters, as sport. The true nature of sports mastery is to fully actualize and totally maximize each athlete's *own* full potential as related and expressed through their sport.

What's Happened to Sports & Athletes Today?

Remember, as professional athletes, we are here to perform our art to the best of our ability, hopefully, while displaying grace, beauty, and heroism. We're here to inspire, so what has happened to sports today? There are many factors that bring about the apathy, lethargy and general negativity associated with pro sports today, but it can be most easily described as ***Sports Dilution.***

What is Sports Dilution?

Dilution of sports in layman terms refers to sports that have become "watered down" or "diluted". The Merriam-Webster New Collegiate Dictionary defines ***dilution*** as; "a lessening of real value by a decrease in relative worth", and another definition states it's meaning as; "to diminish the strength, flavor, or brilliance of something."

Thanks to mass media neuro-programming and cultural changes in the world it seems that sports and its athletes are in many ways completely contradictory to the fundamentals of sports mastery. It appears that many athletes are not only "O.K" with losing once or twice, but losing consistently. Most athletes' today say the same tired, worn out but politically correct, comments after a tough loss, "We're going to try and get better and continue to work on getting better, etc." They act like they want to win but, when it comes down to it, the proof is in the pudding. Judging from their actions and demeanor it seems as if they don't really want or even have the desire to win.

Sad to say, apparent giving up is as commonplace now for many of the so-called "top athletes" than ever before as shown by their ever-prevalent, lackadaisical, pompous, nonchalant attitudes. It must be very difficult to be a true champion and master your sport when all that is focused on is just playing hard enough for an increase in salary or to secure a signing bonus.

Settling for losses, being content with losing on a consistent basis not only goes against sports mastery but against the very philosophy and nature of sport itself. As we stated earlier, the object is to win the game or event and when athletes are not giving their all at a competition or they're "taking the night off" from a game, they are doing fans and other players a terrible disservice. The entire sport becomes tainted and often times, the true winner is never realized.

There seems to be more concern with the image the athlete has or his/her swagger, rather than be focused on substance. What most athletes don't seem to realize is that the best image builder and the best form of currency is to win and win consistently. Everything will take care of itself after that.

Where Have All the Masters Gone?

Is Sports Mastery Dead?

Not by a long shot! I believe mastery is still very much alive in sports today. We just have to filter through the dilution of the current sports world to get to the truth.

In past times, only the truly exceptional professional athletes, both men and women, would be considered heroes and hoisted up on a pedestal. Nowadays, because of mass marketing and media sponsorships, any athlete can be splashed all across the television with or without mastery or a winning philosophy of any kind. In other words, they can be portrayed as champions or masters by the media when in actuality, they're not.

For the true champions and consistent winners, what sets them apart is their commitment to mastery. Athletes guided by sports mastery principles is what makes them who they are and makes them the champions they are; not only their physical, mental or tactical abilities.

Many top athletes today claim to have the desire to reach the highest levels of athletic achievement but, how many have the will to prepare for it? It may seem obvious that most athletes have the will and desire to attain the highest level of athletic achievement, but only those on the path to mastery have the will and desire to prepare for it.

There are top athletes that are indeed on the path to mastery and these are the ones that "stand out". When they perform their art or sport, mastery becomes apparent to the viewers.

We have all watched a sporting event and seen glimpses of greatness and mastery, even if only for a short time.

We've been witness to the pro basketball player who "put the team on his back" and carried them to the championship; or perhaps, the pro quarterback that goes out one afternoon on NFL Sunday and throws 5 touchdowns and no interceptions. Then, there's major league pitcher that throws his 5th consecutive no hitter in a row. How about the professional tennis player that goes from being down two sets and comes back and wins the match. We could go on and on, but it shows that the signs of top performances and athletic achievements are out there, but the consistency and mastery is what's missing.

Sports Mastery is about getting yourself to a point where you consistently perform at a master level. When sports mastery has become your nature you will be able to consistently perform at the master level because that's what you are. A frog doesn't change his nature or being….. he is a frog and frogs do frog things. So, masters do master's things, like winning and consistently performing at the highest levels.

If an athlete becomes a master in his/her sport, plays the game the right way and wins consistently.... what better image builder is there than that?

Unfortunately, many athletes of today who are striving for sports mastery are at a loss because most coaches and trainers don't teach sports mastery......or mastery of any kind for that matter. Standard methods and teachings of peak performance and mental toughness training are the same old, outdated sports principles that prove for most athletes to produce only standard results at best.

Whether you're playing in the Finals, Super Bowl, Wimbledon, World Series, Olympics, or any other major sporting event......standard training and standard results just won't do. You need *sports mastery!*

Is it Possible to Master a Sport?

Can I Really Do It?

In short, I would say, *"Absolutely"!*

Yes, any dedicated athlete can learn to master his/her sport as long as they have the desire and the will to do so. Contrary to popular belief there have been many "masters" in sports already. The greats in sports history have shown us the way to reach the highest levels of athletic achievement and consistently win championships. Coaches can also become masters at coaching in their sport. We've seen legendary coaches throughout history who have obviously, learned to master coaching in their sport. They continually lead their teams to championships.

Michael Jordan stated that once he learned how to incorporate various philosophies and training into his life he then became a "master at the game of basketball." He obviously felt mastery was not only possible; but that he already achieved it.

Every pro athlete will achieve sports mastery at a different rate and it doesn't have to take years and years, although once you are on the path to mastery you will see that it's more of a lifestyle or a way you approach the game. The best part is that many pro athletes are very close to sports mastery already, they may only be missing a few key pieces.

So, the closer you are already, the easier and quicker it will be for you.

Even older athletes are great candidates for sports mastery because of their increased experience in the sport which can many times make a huge difference in the development and progression toward winning championships.

Whether in life, business or sports, all the great thinkers, athletes, educators and business people in our history all agree on this one point…….mastery in all its forms is **Attitude.**

Bestselling author on winning; psychologist Denis Waitley states; *"Your attitude toward your potential is either the key to or the lock on the door of personal fulfillment."*

So, if one of your goals for personal fulfillment is to win the championship, your attitude towards that is the greatest determining factor. You must remember that any sport you are engaged in is led by you which is led by your mind. Therefore, you must realize that your attitude plays a major role in the outcome of your goal.

To date, Lou Holtz is the only college football coach to lead six different programs to bowl games and the only coach to guide four different programs to the final top 20 rankings.

He stated, *"Ability is what you're capable of doing. Motivation determines what you do. Attitude determines how well you do it."*

<u>So, What About Team Sports?</u>

<u>Is it Possible to Master a Team Sport?</u>

Once again, absolutely! Even in team sports each individual can become a master at his/her own position, in addition to applying a team mastery concept. We've all witnessed teams in many different sports who were over-matched athletically or otherwise, and still ended up winning the game or tournament because they played "together" better. What we're saying is that the *synergy* of the team was the key…. not solely, athletic ability.

Research shows that the most successful teams all have at least 4 characteristics that have a direct effect on their success. They all...

Have a meaningful purpose

Have a clear sense of their challenge & future success

Have passion for what they do & the path they're on

Identify the challenge and implement a specific plan driven by determined focus and the pursuit of excellence

We could add another characteristic to the list, and that is each successful team had sense of togetherness and camaraderie that went well beyond that of the competition.

This is where the *coach's mastery* comes into play. Many times, a winning culture and "togetherness" is developed and nurtured by the coach. A coach that applies sports mastery principles can determine the best ways to promote a winning culture while improving team camaraderie. An attribute of a sports mastery minded coach is the ability to help maximize their players potential or "get the best" out of their performances. If every athlete on a team is a master at their position and they are led by a coach that employs a team mastery and synergy concept, can you imagine the potential! That team would obviously be a force to be reckoned with and a formidable opponent.

In an article describing his coaching philosophy, 13-Time Champion Phil Jackson, (11 Championships as a coach, 2 as a player), suggested that *"no team with only a single dominant player can consistently win championships, and that selfish play leads to resentment amongst players and lower team morale. To win championships consistently, as the Celtics, Lakers, and Bulls have done in recent decades, each member of the team must feel valued in a way that facilitates focus on the common goal: winning the game."*

As the philosopher Aristotle once stated regarding sport, *"What's important is for each player to understand his or her proper role or function on the team, and work unstintingly to fulfill that role."*

What is Needed to Master a Sport?

Obviously, every athlete is different, but until we start playing games and holding sporting events with other animals or extraterrestrials, all of us are basically given the same tools to work with; two arms, two legs, two eyes, two ears, etc.

In order to master a sport, all that is needed is the will and desire to do so, a proven system, and an expert in sports mastery to actually show you how to implement the system and help along the way. An athlete on the path to mastery can save lots of time and energy by enlisting the services of a qualified sports mastery artisan.

A sports mastery artisan is an instructor and practitioner that should be able to correct wrong techniques, provide expert problem analysis and suggestions for accelerated results.

Bruce Lee refers to mastery in its purest form as neither a quick fix nor an end result such as a championship; rather an athlete must be committed to the practice of his art, discipline, or sport. Since, true mastery is ever evolving, one must embrace the journey. You need to stop thinking "win the event" or "win the tournament" and start thinking mastery.

Winning consistently or simply winning when it matters most, is not a problem for a sports master. Once you master your sport; you are in total control and if you decide you want to win the championship, it'll be up to you.

So, all that's needed for you to master your sport is you, a proven system, and a sports mastery instructor, called *an artisan*, to help guide you along the way. As long as you have the desire and the will to work at mastering your sport, you can definitely achieve this lofty prize.

Chapter

②

Discover The Proven System

For You To

Master Your Sport,

Win Championships

And Be Etched Into History

As a True Champion

……..In half the time!

What is Your System?

Before we go into your system for achieving sports mastery, it's important that we understand the basic formula that many of the top pro athletes are taught. <u>This is one of the key reasons why most pro athletes never win it all and those that do still never actualize their full sports potential.</u>

You need to seriously think about your current system for achieving mastery. Do you know if you're even followng a system or not? Out of 127 of the great sport masters in our history that we've studied, research shows that every single one had a <u>complete system</u> or blueprint that they followed to reach their highest levels of achievement.

For example, many years ago, a golf magazine published an article regarding a conversation about a young up and coming golfer. The young golfer's caddy was asked his thoughts on winning championships.

In reference to the young golfer, the caddy stated, "*He wants to win major championships, (plural). We just keep plugging along. People just keep doubting him and doubting me as a coach, and we just keep working on our <u>plan</u>.*"

The caddy was Hank Haney, who was Tiger Woods' swing coach.

Before politics, Arnold Schwarzenegger was considered one of the elite training and body building pioneers. He stated, in an article on bodybuilding; *"I realized early the importance of visualization and setting goals. You visualize how you want something to be and then you set goals to achieve it. You devise **a plan** to get there and then work like hell to get there no matter what obstacles get in your way. "*

Michael Johnson, once the world's fastest man, said; *"Really knowing myself allowed me to develop **a plan** that took into account my strengths and my weakness, allowing me to achieve all of my goals."*

All the greats in sports history had specific plans and systems in place to follow, in order to reach their highest levels of achievement. Likewise, you also need a specific plan or system for sports mastery.

Statistics show that most pro athletes don't use any system for reaching their highest levels. Most simply follow their coaches and trainers instruction, which may or may not be the best thing. Every athlete needs a good coach, but most coaches and trainers never even consider sports mastery as the means for winning championships, let alone teach a system or a method for attaining it. So, it would be a good idea for you to consider the system and advice you are following.

How can you expect to reach your highest level of sports mastery and win championships consistently if you are not being trained <u>for</u> mastery? If you are following a system to just "make you a better player" or to make you "perform better", you may want to explore other options more geared towards sports mastery. In order to reach the highest level and actualize your full sports potential, you need a system focused on achieving sports mastery.

The Foundation: Sports Mastery Model

To identify the foundation, we will go back to psychology 101 and look to some of the great theorists of our time. One theorist, Abraham Maslow suggested a model listing the needs that must be met for human progression on a personal level with the prize of self-actualization being at the top. This model has since been known as ***Maslow's Hierarchy of Needs.***

Many great theorists and psychoanalysts such as Goldstein, Rogers and Jung have all used self-actualization in various psychology theories in slightly different ways, but Maslow's hierarchy of needs is what brought the concept to prominence. They all do agree, however, on the same basic concept of self-actualization as the full realization of one's potential. Once self-actualization is reached the person would be able to maximize his/her potential and achieve their highest goals.

Maslow's original hierarchy lists some basic needs that need to be met in order to progress on a personal level. He suggested that once these needs are met, then an individual is primed for self-actualization. (See Fig. 1-a.)

(Fig. 1-a.) *Maslow's Hierarchy of Needs*

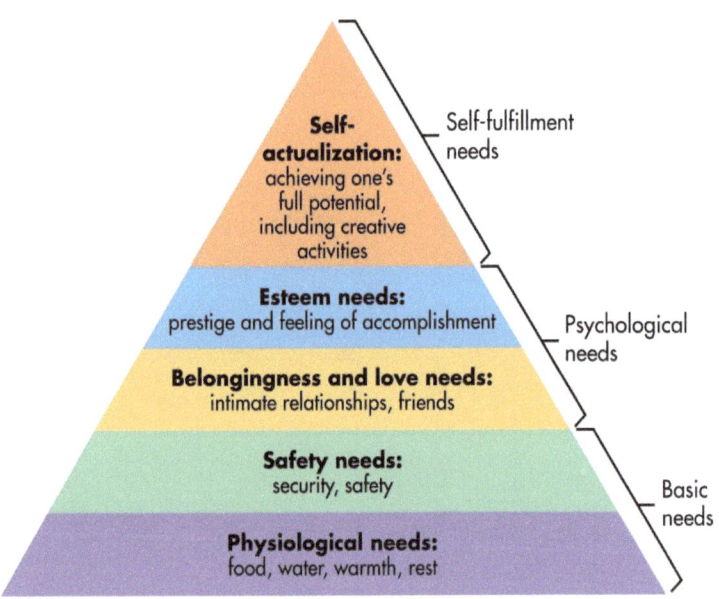

Self-actualization was to be the supreme level of being on a personal level. A person would be able to tap into his/her full potential once this level is reached and virtually nothing would be impossible for them to achieve.

Abraham Maslow developed the Hierarchy of Needs model in the mid 1900's, and his theory remains valid today as an aid to understanding human development and can be aptly applied to athletes and sports. His and other great thinkers' concepts on self-actualization can be applied to pro athletes in the sports world. If self actualization is the highest personal level that we should strive to reach, then sports mastery would be the highest level for the pro athlete.

The Typical Pro Athlete Training Model

Being that most coaches and trainers have never even considered sports mastery as the means for winning championships; one may wonder, <u>what system are they teaching then?</u>

If most professional athletes today are, in fact, taught a method or system for reaching the highest levels of winning, it is obviously filled with many holes and gaps, which is why so many of our top athletes come to the end angry, frustrated and embarrassed by heart breaking losses.

If any athlete, even a top superstar, is taught a system filled with holes and gaps, it will show in their performance and results. The athlete's "game" will be filled with holes and gaps as well.

With Maslow's hierarchy in mind, here is what the typical pro athletes training model for sports mastery would look like. (See fig.1-b)

Fig. 1-b. Typical Professional Athlete Mode

According to Maslow's hierarchy, reaching one's full potential or self actualization is at the top of the model.

Now, it may be said that every athlete, coach or trainer is obviously looking to reach the highest levels of achievement, but it is very difficult to actually do this when you follow a model that's filled with holes. Because this is happening across all sports without bias, it is how we come to realize the true nature of the typically flawed pro athlete model.

Holes and Gaps

Let's look at why the typical pro athlete model for winning rarely ever works. One reason comes from an idea that has been erroneously conveyed often by so called "experts." The idea that, "Physically, most athletes are in top condition. The difference can be found in their mental status." As one highly regarded coach put it; "The difference between a good athletic performance and an outstanding one has little to do with physical skills…. everyone's game is good at the pro level, so it's psychological factors that makes most of the difference."

While mental training is indeed essential, that statement is only a half truth at best. This type of reasoning is why you most likely have holes and gaps in *your* game now! There are many, many different factors a pro athlete needs to consider in order to reach the highest levels of achievement and sports mastery.

Yes, pro athletes are in top condition, relative to normal people, but once you take a microscopic look into a pro athletes' world, you'll find there is a huge disparity between them across many different areas, not just the mental aspect.

We have all seen athlete's win games or events because they showed up in better physical shape than their opponent. We've also seen athlete's lose games, for the same reason. Likewise, we've seen athlete's known for being mentally tough and "clutch-players" win it all when it counted most. We've also seen super star athletes known for being mentally tough and "clutch-players" fold up when it counted most and lose in the big game.

These types of training programs, ones that address only one portion or another, is why so many of our super star athletes, even at their high level, never even scratch the surface of their true potential.

You need a system that addresses **all** the needs of the pro athlete and is laser focused towards sports mastery. Out of 127 of the greatest sport masters in our history, research showed that every single one had a <u>complete</u> system that they followed to reach their highest levels of achievement.

Obviously, the differences in the pro athletes that consistently win championships are not solely in the physical or mental aspect; rather, it lies in their philosophy or system they use to approach their sport and their commitment to the plan. This, in turn, yields the edge in physical and mental capabilities as well as performance.

Judging from the typical pro athletic model for winning, apparently, it is based on a very simple recipe: Develop the physical body… Develop the mental toughness….Practice your butt off in your sport….Keep repeating until desired results are achieved.

That recipe may be of use at certain levels but, not so much at the professional level of sports and sad to say, this is the model that most pro athletes are taught to follow.

By following this model, it becomes apparent why sports dilution has occurred and why so many top athletes are constantly experiencing the embarrassment and frustration of losing. If every athlete uses that same flawed system, everyone will be basically the same, with everyone performing their sport at less than mastery levels and all having flawed, hole-filled games. You need a system that addresses **all** the needs of the pro athlete and is laser focused towards sports mastery.

<u>*The Real System for Sports Mastery*</u>

We will no doubt agree that actualization or sports mastery is what every serious athlete should work towards, but in order to reach mastery, you need a system that is specifically designed for mastery.

An ideal system for mastery should have a model that is based on scientific theory and principles, actual player trial and error application, and experiences from sports masters who have already used the system to win championships and have created their legacies.

By modeling and researching the greats and what they've taught us, use of a hierarchical model similar to Maslow's with sports mastery as the apex, should be the basis for the evolution of the athletes' journey. The only sports mastery model for pro sports found today was developed by my leading human performance and actualization research company, "Psionova". Here is an example of what has come to be known as *The Psionovan Sports Mastery Model*. (See Fig. 1-c)

Fig. 1-c Psionovan Pro Sports Mastery Model

It should now be clear to see why the typical pro athletic model is flawed. The typical pro athlete' sports model uses a basic recipe of physical training combined with mental toughness and skilled practice with no mention of sports mastery or even reaching the highest level at all.

The Psionovan Sports Mastery Model addresses all of the pro athletes needs to achieve sports mastery. The model focuses on experiential needs, physical and mental conditioning, moral and esteem needs and synergistically ties them all together for mastery using their proprietary A.M.A.S.S. System.

In order for you to reach sports mastery you need to leverage the power of Psionova's Athletic Mastery & Sports Synergy System (A.M.A.S.S. ™).

This system is specifically designed for any pro athlete to achieve mastery in their given sport in the shortest amount of time possible. The power and effectiveness of the A.M.A.S.S. system lies in its **Deep Analysis & Progression Instrument** (D.A.P.I.) and the **True Champion Attributes Formula** (T.C.A.F.).

The Psionovan system for sports mastery uses its deep analysis assessment for each athlete that is then cross referenced against 47 championship indexes to find the holes and gaps in the professional athletes' game. The A.M.A.S.S.

system will then generate each athlete their own specific, customized blueprint for sports mastery.

Since, sports mastery is a relatively new concept, the proprietary A.M.A.S.S. system should only be taught by and learned from a qualified sports mastery instructor called an *artisan*. For more information on how you can crush your competition and dominate your sport through mastery, and my detailed breakdown of The Psionovan Sports Mastery Model, contact us at http://psionova.com.

How to Get Results in Half the Time?

How Do You Accelerate Progress?

Malcolm Gladwell dedicates a chapter from his best-selling book, "Outliers", to the concept that "ten thousand hours of practice is required to achieve the level of mastery associated with being a world-class expert....in anything."

To further understand the 10,000 hours concept, neurologist Daniel Levitin spells it out in Outliers: *"In study after study; composers, basketball players, fiction writers, ice skaters, concert pianists, chess players, master criminals, and what have you….. this number comes up again and again. Of course, this doesn't address why some people get more out of their practice sessions than others do, but no one has yet found a case in which true world-class expertise was accomplished in less time. It seems that it takes the brain that long to assimilate all that it needs to know about how to achieve true mastery."*

We are constantly doing further research into this but, it seems that the 10,000 hour concept does have some validity. The good thing for the professional athlete is that this is covered in the sports mastery model. Remember, the 10,000 hours may look big and frightening at first, but it's tiny when you want to master something you are passionate about. You could master sports, music, dance, computers, art--- or anything you are truly dedicated and passionate about and never know how you passed those hours.

For a professional athlete who has competed, practiced and trained for many years….this 10,000th mark was most likely surpassed a long time ago. Even, if we just think in your normal athletic course of things; years of high school, college, and pro practices and games, you've probably reached that number a while ago. However, what has not been said is how many may have reached that number of hours put in and still haven't achieved the results they needed.

The easiest way to accelerate your progress and get the results you want in half the time is to enlist the services of a qualified sports mastery artisan. At the pro level, you have, no doubt, already logged in many hours worth of practice and training so, it's a good idea for virtually every athlete to have an outside coach/mentor. Your sports mastery artisan can save you time and energy because he/she can help you put it *all* together. Your artisan has actually competed in high level sports in this era and will fully understand the nature of the game as it is played and felt **today**, not 20, 30 or more years ago.

Your artisan should have experience actually implementing principles personally within his/her own sport, therefore they can point out ways to save you time and energy, too.

A sports mastery artisan has the ability and energy to actually roll up his/her sleeves and get into your sport with you and not only "tell" you but, *actually show* you specific tips and techniques for mastery of your sport. Your sports mastery artisan should also be able to guide you along your path to mastery and provide sound advice, suggestions and shortcuts to dramatically accelerate your progress.

As with team sports, you obviously need your team to practice with, but every athlete still needs their own private, (outside the Organization), mentor and consultant. A sports mastery artisan will be able to instruct and guide individual athletes, as well as teams.... including coaches, staff members and upper management.

Professional team coaches and trainers need outside consultation and even though most organizations provide additional coaches and trainers, you must realize it is still within the confines of the organization and not beyond a measure of bias, capability, honesty and control. That is why an outside, honest, objective, expert analysis, **with a solution**, is needed. If you are a coach or trainer and need to revamp your system or coaching philosophy, feel free to contact Psionova and get your team on the path to sports mastery.

Chapter ③

Right and Wrong

Training Methods:

Little Pointers

That Will Have You

Holding Up Your Trophy

This Year!

Many athletes think that wrong training techniques only refer to bad form and/or technique during physical exercise...... but, the records show that many of these wrong training practices come from the mind. This would include the "wrong" perspective learned from the teachings of an incomplete or an improper system.

Once you have started your journey to sports mastery, you will undoubtedly have questions or concerns and the consultation of a qualified sports mastery expert is advised.

Keeping that in mind, let's address some of the right and wrong training techniques being used by top professional athletes today for attaining the highest levels of achievement.

Attack of the Clones

We've already stated the pitfalls of following a cookie cutter plan or a hole-filled system, but, in my humble opinion one of the main or primarily used wrong training techniques is not even following any system or plan at all!

If you wanted to be a world class body builder, you wouldn't just go into the gym and say I want to look like Arnold Schwarzenegger and just start working out. You need a specific plan to get you from where you are now, to where you want to be. The only plan most pro athletes are taught to follow is no more than a glorified plan to get stronger, run faster or jump higher.

These types of peak performances and performance enhancement programs are obviously useful for sports, but, are only focusing on a portion of what the pro athlete needs to reach sports mastery. If your plan is to only improve your physical ability, then we can see.... there will be many areas that are left unaddressed.

After you've gotten stronger and faster, then what? How will you be able to correlate that into your sport when practices are not enough? I'm certain, all of us have seen top athletes that are extremely gifted physically or are in top physical condition but still were not that great "at their sport." We constantly see top pro athletes who are super fast or super strong and still lose in the end, when it counts the most. Enough is enough.

Aren't We All the Same? Isn't Everybody Equal?

Another wrong training technique seems to stem from an idea that has been conveyed often by many, so- called "experts". The idea goes something like, "Physically, most athletes are in top condition, the main difference can be found in their mental status." This is only a half truth at best and this type of reasoning is why **you** most likely have holes and gaps in your game, now!

Many our top athletes have had the "mental toughness" and the confidence to win, but still lost in the big games! We've seen it time and time again, and across all sports; super star athletes beat on their chest and yell and scream with emotion and confidence, obviously being mentally tough and still not perform well and lose the game or event. Most of the legends in sports history all had a supreme level of mental toughness, confidence and courage, but, that's not **all** they had. They were complete athletes…..sports masters!

Loser's Mentality

In recent times, stemming from consistent losses, there seems to be a more and more prevalent mentality…. "losing is OK". This losing mentality has come to be so commonplace that we now hear clichés like, "on any given Sunday, *anybody can win or lose*"…. alluding to the fact that it's **OK,** when you lose because you have no control over the outcome anyway.

Or, when you know failure is a possibility, you may tell yourself (and others) excuses or reasons why you are not at your best, such as:

"I'm injured and not at full strength……. that's why I lost"

"I'm still fatigued from the last game or event!"

"They have a <u>stacked </u>team!"

"The opponent has always been better!"

And my personal favorite……*"I'm still kinda messed up from partying last night."*

These types of excuses sports psychology refers to as **self-handicapping,** but no matter the term, it still plays into the loser's mentality.

We hear these self-handicapping excuses all the time. Basically, it's just people trying to justify to themselves and others that if the conditions were different, they would succeed. Essentially, they blame the *potential* loss, on circumstances, not themselves. For these reasons, sports masters never bother with a loser's mentality, rather they safeguard themselves from it.

Key Components from Champions' Training

The following are a few of the key components that have been extrapolated from years of research on the best training regimens, by some of sports historical champions.

Two of the main commonalities we find between these champions are that of their ***mental preparation*** and their ***approach*** to their training and sport.

Belief – You Gotta Believe To Achieve

As of November 2011, tennis great, Roger Federer has won a men's record of 16 Grand Slam singles titles and a record

6 ATP World Tour Finals and 18 ATP Masters Series tournaments (second all-time). During his press conferences in the end of year 2006, Masters in Shanghai , Roger Federer finally explained the one major thing which turned his career around.

Earlier, he regularly lost to the top players such as Lleyton Hewitt, who at that time was the number one player in the world, and to tough opponents like Andy Roddick. His secret sounds so simple yet it made all the difference to his career. Federer said his career finally went golden when he learned not to panic on the court when he was down or under pressure and instead of giving up, he now "hangs in there and hopes for the best whenever things are down." He would not give up when the "chips were down" but instead he would "**believe**" that he could still win.

Federer may have been losing in many matches, but ended up victorious. Federer attributes his success to this one simple decision, and said it has been the best choice that he has ever made in tennis career.

One could say that Federer wins many matches because of the amount of inner belief he has from the incredible win/loss record he amassed from 2003-2006. The fact is that he did not begin to amass this record until he first began <u>believing in himself</u>.

Federer realized that, in order to become a champion, he had to first begin thinking like one. This made all the difference in his career. This is actually the opposite of how most athletes and coaches think. Most believe that once they start winning a lot, <u>then</u> the confidence and belief will come, which will help them in turn keep winning.

Scientific evidence and research shows that this is not how it works. As with Federer, he discovered it's actually the other way around. The secret is that you have to first create the belief <u>before</u> you will begin winning.

"You know, I saw myself on the 18th green lifting the trophy and it's almost something that you already believe." – **Lorena Ochoa,** first Mexican-born player to win on the L.P.G.A. Tour.

"You must <u>expect</u> great things of yourself <u>before</u> you can do them". – **Michael Jordan,** (6-Time NBA Champion, 5-Time Season MVP, 3-Time Finals MVP)

Visualize – See It and Achieve It

Visualization is where you can see yourself in your mind, already accomplishing your goal. This is powerful because as stated earlier, your mind has to first be able to see your goal in order to be able to achieve it.

You must create a mental model to focus on, a complete technique, or a specific action, for example: your arm swinging the tennis racket and executing a blazing fast serve or your leg kicking a soccer ball or you shooting a perfect jumper.

You need to have an intent, but relaxed focus coupled with repeated study of the specific actions. Focus on your body position, power, speed, stamina and breathing. Replay the mental movie many times. Close your eyes and visualize this using your mind's eye. Run the movie in your mind just prior to performing the activity. Feel the energy in your muscles, and then put yourself into the actions displayed in your mental movie.

"My entire physique and all my physique titles came as a result of visualization and goal setting". **Arnold Schwarzenegger,** (5 Time Mr. Universe & 7 Time Mr. Olympia)

Legendary educator Napoleon Hill said, *"Whatever your mind can conceive and believe, it can achieve."* This also holds true in sports. If you believe or in your mind's eye you can "see" yourself mastering your sport then you can definitely become a master in your sport.

"Visualization was the key to my success." - **Jack Nicklaus,** (Winner of 6 Masters and a record 18 Majors)

"When I train, one of the things I concentrate on is creating a mental picture of how best to deliver that ball to a teammate, preferably leaving him alone in front of the rival goalkeeper. So what I do....always before a game -- always, every night and every day -- is try and think up things, imagine plays, which no one else will have thought of, and to do so, always bearing in mind the particular strengths of each teammate to whom I am passing the ball. When I construct those plays in my mind, I take into account whether one teammate likes to receive the ball at his feet or ahead of him, if he's good with his head and how he prefers to head the ball or, if he's stronger on his right or his left foot. That's my job! That is what I do. I imagine the game." - **Cristiano Ronaldinho,** (Brazilian soccer player, currently considered one of the world's best)

Know Thyself

"Whether you train with a power tap or heart rate monitor or another device.... that's all well and good, but you need to be able to control your own effort and your own intensity and internalize that race pace, so when you get onto the course, <u>you know</u> what pace <u>you</u> can sustain. When everything's hurting 30K into the marathon, no heart rate monitor is going to help you." – **Chrissie Wellington,** (British Triathlete and triple World Ironman Champion 2007, 2008, 2009)

She goes on to say, "It's important to hurt in training and to learn to suffer a bit. Embrace fatigue and pain—welcome it and develop strategies to embrace it. If it doesn't hurt, you're not working hard enough. You're not always going to have easy days in training—you're going to be frustrated and have a bad day and it's important to learn to endure those in training. When you experience it in a race, you've already encountered it and can have that peace of mind."

"How" to Train Like a Champion

Training beyond your capabilities is the only way to get better and **the champions** and **the sports masters** in history have all known this. Here are some thoughts from some of the top athletes.

"Some people train to win. I train to eliminate the possibility of defeat." – **Sir Steve Redgrave,** (5 time Olympic Gold Medalist Rowing, 1984, 1988, 1992, 1996, 2000 – Great Britain)

"There are no shortcuts. You can't cut corners. You can't cheat. You have to stay focused on your goals, and you have to do all your drills." – **Carl Lewis,** (9 Time Olympic Gold Medalist & 8 Time World Championship Gold Medalist)

"I made it look so easy on the court all those years. No one realized how hard I had to work. No one realized how much I had to put into it. They underestimated my intensity." - **Pete Sampras,** (14-Time Grand Slam Tournament Winner)

Determination & Commitment

"You just can't beat the person who never gives up."- **Babe Ruth,** (7 time World Series Champion and 2-Time All-Star)

"Unless a man believes in himself and makes a total commitment to his career and puts everything he has into it….his mind, his body, his heart…..what's life worth to him." - **Vince Lombardi,** (5 time NFL Champion)

"Sustained excellence is achieved through habit and repetition."- **Aristotle**

Focus

"He focused hard. He was more business than flash. I also think he didn't want to look back on his career and have any regrets." – **Pete Sampras,** speaking on Andre Agassi, (8 Grand Slam Titles)

"Focus completely on making your muscles work in perfecting your technique, so that you have maximum efficiency from the lifting muscles you employ. Think of yourself as a finely-tuned athlete with smooth, flawless, efficient lifting technique." - **Tamio "Tommy" Kono** (3-Time Olympic Medalist Weightlifter, the only lifter to have set world records in four different weightlifting classes)

"I've talked to a lot of successful people around the game, and that's what they all have in common; they stay focused every single day." – **Shelley Duncan,** (2007 rookie of the New York Yankees speaking on Mark McGwire and other baseball heavy hitters)

"The source of unshakable confidence in sport is having the RIGHT FOCUS. When you have the RIGHT FOCUS in training, you make major leaps in your skill development. When you have the RIGHT FOCUS in competition, you make excellent decisions, which leads to peak performance and winning. Peak performance gives you unshakable confidence…..the conviction that you can cope with the challenges of competition." – **Dr. Lisa Lane Brown,** (author and coach)

<u>Nutrition</u>

Let's not forget about nutrition. In order to reach your highest levels of achievement you will need to use proper nutrition as a way to optimize your athletic performance from the inside-out.

Improving athletic performance, reducing injury, knowing when, what and how often to eat, (and drink), is one of the best kept secrets in the sports industry. As you and your training evolve you will need adequate proteins, carbohydrates, fats, and fluids to satisfy your body's needs.

A good multi-vitamin and mineral supplement can also help with your nutritional requirement. Nutrition can have a dramatic impact on an athlete's development. A top professional athlete on the path to sports mastery will need a customized training program supported by proper nutrition.

Now that you know the system you need and have learned some basic concepts from previous champions, you are no doubt ready to begin on your path to sports mastery. Let's find out how to prepare to quickly and easily absorb your new system for winning.

Chapter

Your Pre-Mastery Warm up:

How To Prepare Yourself

To Quickly Absorb

A

New

Revolutionary

System For Winning

Preparation is Key

One of the foundational building blocks for sports mastery is preparation. You don't just show up on game day without putting your body through intense training first. Your training sessions are basically the preparations for the real game or event. So, one of the first steps to being a sports master is to prepare yourself for sports mastery.

When asked about the great John Wooden's approach on the preparation it took that resulted in multiple NCAA basketball championships, a former player stated, *"He never talked about winning. The only thing we can control is our preparation. So focused was Wooden, on preparing his teams on fundamentals from the ground up, that he began each season by teaching his players the proper way to put on their socks."*

In a New York Times article with Olympic athletes discussing great accomplishments and why tremendous preparation is necessary, one such athlete stated, *"The first thing you see in all these cases is the overwhelming confidence that intense preparation brings about. I know what that's like. When you're on your game and you know that everybody else knows it* too....it's a big psychological advantage." - **Eric Heiden,** (Won five gold medals in a sweep of the individual men's speed skating events during the 1980 Olympics)

Feeling the Flow

The first step in preparation begins in your mind and then must be channeled with a concrete game plan. Your success depends on your ability to acknowledge your dream and then take action on your dream.

In sports, athletes often refer to their supreme feeling as being in the "Zone". Eastern philosophers experience similar meditative states when practicing *Zen Buddhism*. Scientists and renowned psychologists call this "flow."

Flow is the term coined by University of Chicago Psychologist Mihaly Csikszentmihalyi, (1990) to refer to this psychological dimension described by thousands of individuals during his 25 years of researching this universal phenomenon. He suggested that during flow, consciousness becomes harmoniously ordered and this is the state of being you want to be in before you begin implementing your blueprint for sports mastery.

According to Daniel Goleman, author of Emotional Intelligence, the ability to enter a state of flow represents emotional intelligence at its best, because it is incompatible with emotional discord or strain. Flow is considered an autotelic, or intrinsically rewarding experience. Since it feels so good, this optimal experience becomes not just a means, but an end in itself.

Usually for pro athletes, getting into the "the zone" or "putting your game face on", is something reserved only for pre-game or pre-competition preparation. While this is indeed helpful, sports masters know that the same approach and mentality needs to be employed regarding <u>every</u> training session.

This means that you need to get yourself in a state of being or feeling that is optimal for training, whether it be physical or mental training.

One of the easiest ways to get the most out of any training is to have your mind and body "primed" to receive the training you are about to give it. You will greatly benefit from using this one simple practice before training. It's shocking how many top pro athletes actually just "go" into the gym, workout and then expect the best results. You can easily maximize the results you get from every training exercise by utilizing the well known physiological principle of *maximum absorption*.

Sports mastery suggests that athletes' should get into the maximum absorption state, (M.A.), before every serious training session. The beauty of flow or being in the "zone" is that it automatically puts you in the max absorption state. All aspects of the athlete's total being should be in this maximum absorption state in order to reap the full benefits from <u>every</u> training session. When you are in the M.A. state, every single aspect of your training session will be fully absorbed and therefore can be fully synthesized and then maximized.

<u>How do I get into the M.A. State?</u>

Getting into the M.A. state is easy. You have to do things that get you to feel good, comfortable and relaxed, while still being energetic, motivated, and excited. You already know that in order to take full advantage of any training program or instruction you first need to get yourself in the proper state of being or feeling. Since, every athlete is different it is important to follow a plan that is customized specifically for you and taking into account your personal preferences for getting into the max absorption state.

Visualization practices are an easy way to get yourself prepared and ready to absorb the system for achieving sports mastery. Here are some quick ways to use visualization to help get you into the max absorption state.

Quick Visualization Tips

Your visualization starts at the beginning of a routine or workout. Start by taking 2 or 3 deep breaths in and out to relax yourself. You can close your eyes or keep them open while doing this, whatever feels best for you. You need to think about what results you are aiming for. Get a clear picture of your goal in your mind. To assist you, it may be a good idea to even write down your goal and keep it in a place where you can see it and refer to it often.

While in a relaxed state, picture the whole routine of your workout in as much detail as possible. Visualize the area, the weather, or feeling in the room, the temperature, the sounds, the smells--everything. Imagine yourself warming up, stretching, talking to friends, concentrating…everything you do when you are about to compete or work out. The main thing is to get yourself into a state of being where you are feeling relaxed and ready at the same time.

Imagine yourself beginning your workout. Notice everything you do and see it perfectly just the way you want it to be done. If you make a mistake while visualizing your performance, go back, slow down the image in your mind, and do it over again, correctly. Experience yourself achieving your goal. Try and "feel" what it's like when you perform well.

"Before training or competing, you must take the body from a resting state to a working state. Jog at least two laps, then stretch. He does only a few standing stretches. That's just personal preference. Do as much or as little as you need to feel comfortable." - (Former running coach for Carl Lewis)

We have all experienced the feeling where we were having a "bad day" or today we just don't "feel it", but these are the types of feelings you want to avoid before beginning any serious training. It will be very difficult to get maximum results from any training session when you are feeling less than optimal, which is why it is very important to get into the correct state before your training sessions. Think back to the last time you performed well or were in a zone. Can you remember how good it felt? If so, try and replicate that feeling before and during your training sessions.

Chapter ⑤

How To Create

The Mindset Of

Muhammad Ali, Michael Jordan

And Bruce Lee

……..All In One!

One of the first things that became clearly evident while researching the greatest sports masters in history is their mindset. The attitude, confidence, intelligence, mental toughness and motivation of **the greats** were extraordinary and serve as a perfect example for all top athletes today.

Extensive research shows that every sports master had a supreme image of themselves. This is known as ***self-image***. Your self-image is the mental picture of yourself, which can culminate in different ways. Usually a person's self-image results from the way others see you, the way you "think" other people view you, and/or the way you view yourself. One part of your visualization practice that you need to incorporate is working on your self-image. You need to have in your mind a clear and vivid picture of yourself….. ***as a master in your sport***. This will serve as a mental guide along your path to sports mastery.

Now regarded as "The Greatest", boxing champion and legend Muhammad Ali once stated: *"I am the astronaut of boxing. Joe Louis and Dempsey were just jet pilots. I'm in a world of my own. "* He went on to say: *"I am the greatest! I said that even before I knew I was."* The supreme self-image he had was clear.

How to Get the Sports Masters' Mindset

The aspects of the sports master's mindset; attitude, confidence, mental toughness, etc., all come from your belief and reassurance that comes from your training. You have confidence because you know you put the work in, done your homework and if your training was first class you will no doubt have and "feel" the confidence. Here is a look into the necessary mindset needed for mastery and the actions that you must take to achieve this.

Important Attitudes to Consider

One attitude that can be an impediment to success is self-doubt. There have been many sports psychologists that claim that self-doubt really is your friend. Why? They claim it demonstrates that you are really going after your big dream.

Supposedly, doubt that reflects your purpose, your passion, and your love is what is found in one's heart. So, the premise is that if your dream is so big, that even you doubt your own ability to attain it, then you're on the right track.

Sports masters would disagree however. It may be advantageous to set big goals and dreams that stretch your boundaries, but you should never doubt that you can reach them. When you are first creating your big dream or goal in your mind, it is sometimes normal to *initially,* doubt your ability to reach it. That thought should quickly be released. You should never doubt your own ability to accomplish your goals. Likewise, you should never dwell on your inability to do or reach anything.

Another attitude that some athletes report as being an "enemy of success" is *fear.* Fear in and of itself is not necessarily a bad thing. You have to understand that fear is a tool.

Like any tool, it can be used for positive ends or negative self-defeating ends. Many shamans say that fear is good because it checks the angry spirit. Some fighters have stated that fear, when controlled, helps keep you sharp and alert. However, when fear is left unchecked it can consume you and become your biggest detriment. You must face your fears, learn to control your fears and not let them consume you.

Once you have reached mastery and you control your fears, they will cease to be a concern.

To paraphrase from former president Franklin D. Roosevelt's famous quote: ***"The only thing we have to <u>fear</u>….is fear itself."***

To unlock your sports master mindset you only need your action-driven blueprint to dissolve resistance and propel yourself forward in light speed with a game plan to ensure your success on two important mental levels. This begins with success….. first at the ***belief level***, (your attitude), and secondly, at the ***implementation level***.

We've already stated the importance of your beliefs. You have to <u>believe</u> that you will win multiple championships. You also have to <u>believe</u> that you will reach sports mastery in order for any positive results to transpire.

Secondly, your attitude should be focused on getting the precise instruction you need to reach sports mastery and then applying it. Your attitude should be something like, ***"Please show me exactly what I must do to implement a successful strategy that will unlock my full potential and allow me to reach sports mastery."*** With this proven system, you will reach sports mastery faster than anyone previously.

"You can't outperform your self-image." – Dennis Connor, (American Yachtsman; won the bronze medal at the 1976 Olympics, two Star World Championships, and four wins in the America's Cup)

For an example of the power of dreaming big and setting big goals, we can reference Olympic short skater Apolo Ohno. In his book; "Zero Regrets", he points out that this is the key to achieving your dreams.

Over a decade ago, he wrote, *"I want seven world championships, six gold medals and to be a legend in speed skating."*

He now has eight world championships, eight Olympic medals, (two of them gold), and is regarded as the most decorated U.S. Winter Olympian. To top it off, he even won on the popular TV show "Dancing with the Stars!" With his 8 medals, (two gold, two silver, four bronze), in the Winter Olympics, he is now recognized as the most decorated American Winter Olympic athlete of all time.

In an excerpt from the 2008 New York Times Play Magazine, one of the great soccer players of our time stated, *"I know when I should pass the ball, dribble or shoot. When I have the ball at my feet, I know that something good will emerge. I am always confident."*- Cristiano Ronaldo, a believer in deliberate practice and anticipation skills is factored in his extreme confidence and his recent success.

One of the greatest women's tennis players in history is Billie Jean King. She won 12 Grand Slam singles titles, 16 Grand Slam women's doubles titles, and 11 Grand Slam mixed doubles titles. She even won "The Battle of the Sexes" in 1973, in which she defeated Bobby Riggs, a former Wimbledon men's singles champion, for $100,000, winner take all!

When asked about the mental qualities of champions, King recounts her own tennis experiences by stating, *"The difference between me at my peak and me in the last few years of my career is that when I was the champion I had the ultimate in confidence. When I decided, under pressure ... that I had to go with my very weakest shot, (forehand down the line). I was positive that I could pull it off ... when it mattered most. Even more than that, going into a match, I knew it was my weakest shot, and I knew in a tight spot my opponent was going to dare me to hit it, and I knew I could hit it those two or three or four times in a match when I absolutely had to."* - Billie Jean King

She goes on to state, *"the cliché is to say that champions play the big points better. Yes, but that's only the half of it. The champions play their weaknesses better."*

When asked about the mental toughness and motivation needed to accomplish great things, arguably the greatest professional basketball player ever, Michael Jordan, recounted his own experiences and had this to say;

"You had all the media naysayers...you know, scoring champion can't win the NBA title..., You're not as good as Magic Johnson; You're not as good as Larry Bird. You're good, but you're not as good as those guys. I had to listen to all this, and that put so much wood on that fire... It kept me each and every day, trying to get better as a basketball player... And for someone like me, who achieved a lot...you look for any kind of messages to keep you motivated to play the game of basketball."

Have you ever felt upset or disgruntled with your teammates, coaches, or trainers? Maybe you have even caught yourself criticizing others? Have you ever thought about why you felt that way? What is the root cause of criticizing others?

This is important to consider, because every single one of us has been put down and let down by others and felt the shame and humiliation of it.

Michael Jordan says, *"Channel your frustration. Channel your anger. Let it drive you towards excellence, towards who you really are. But equally important is summoning the mental toughness to display the will to win. When you do, you give courage to your teammates. This is what the word 'en-courage' means – to give courage to. The truth is, it takes guts to stand out from the crowd and aspire greatness. You may face judgment, envy, and even outright rejection from people who witness your greatness first hand."*

One of the greatest martial artists of all time was Bruce Lee. In his book, the Tao of Jeet Kune Do he states, *"Forget about winning and losing, forget about pride and pain. Ideas are the beginning of all achievements."* He further states, *"Knowing is not enough; we must apply. Willing is not enough; we must do."*

The point is that no matter if you face criticism or not, you still need to have the attitude, confidence and mental toughness to withstand the negativity and still drive toward your goal of sports mastery. Make no mistake, there may be many critics and doubters during your evolution, but as you get more in touch with your inner master you will quickly silence them all.

"Not one aspect of your training is as important as motivation. In fact, nothing else is even close. With enough motivation, you will succeed at some level. It's the one ingredient that assures success and, when lacking, will lead to failure." – Lance Armstrong (7 Time Tour de France Winner)

We can all see the benefits to employing mental toughness training and conditioning to your routine but that is still only a portion of the sports master's mindset. What many mental toughness coaches fail to realize is that not only were the great champions mentally tough, they were also extremely intelligent in regards to their sport or martial art. Contrary to many "expert" mental conditioning trainers, mental toughness is not <u>the</u> solution. Indeed it is a part of the solution but there is still much more needed for sports mastery.

We have all seen many times, where a mentally tough athlete doesn't get the job done. Maybe you have experienced this yourself, I know I have. I've been in games and events where I was mentally tough, had the confidence and desire to win, but still didn't perform the best I could have. My mind knew what I wanted to do, (at least, I thought so at the time), but my body wasn't physically ready and able to perform the tasks. This is why peak performance training or mental toughness training by themselves won't get it done. This is because it still is only addressing a part of the whole.

As long as you are only addressing certain pieces; the whole will never come together. Make sure you are following a plan specifically designed for <u>you</u> that will address the whole process for achieving sports mastery. Now, discover the foundation to maximizing your full athletic potential.

Chapter

Discover The Secret Foundation

To Maximize

Your Full Athletic Potential

– Train Like A Master –

Save Months

Of Time And Energy

Wasted On

Peak Performance Training!

Many people believe that the top athletes reach the highest levels simply because they are superb physical specimens. While this is true in many cases, you need to keep in mind that some of the top physical specimens in sports history were also some of the hardest workers. It's no surprise that maximum results and hard work go hand in hand.

An attribute of training like a master is not only training hard and for maximum results, but also, to train in the most efficient ways possible. You must also keep in mind any weaknesses or holes in your game already must be turned into your strengths. By training in an efficient manner you will save time, energy and greatly reduce the risk of injury. You need to train hard, but more importantly, you need to train smart.

"You have to be prepared to be objective and honest about weaknesses and where you can improve and learn from your mistakes. That's how you grow." – Chrissie Wellington – (Triathlete and Four-time World Ironman Champion - 2007, 2008, 2009, 2011)

Training vs. Exercise vs. Working Out

The first way to train like a master is to start thinking like one. You have to be physically prepared, warmed up, for intense training. Likewise, you must be mentally prepared for intense training. Many pro athletes have training programs and trainers to help them implement these techniques. The problem is that even some of the top super star athletes are still only exercising or working out at best.

One thing research has shown concerning sports mastery is that nearly all the masters have a very different outlook on their conditioning than most pro athletes. They usually speak of their conditioning and work out sessions as training. They rarely ever "exercised" or called it "exercising" or "working out". This may seem like an over-simplification but it's well worth examining further.

So what's the difference?

You have to understand that training does require exercises; so what we are really talking about is the mindset.
When you train, you are more focused, determined and serious about your regimen. Also, when you train or, are in

training you are working toward a clearly specified goal, in this case would be sports mastery.

Now, you can exercise all you want, (and many do), with no clear goals or intentions other than general improved physical fitness, but that won't get you to sports mastery. So, as you evolve on your own path to sports mastery it would be a good practice to start thinking of your sessions and regimens as ***training.***

As far as "working out" goes, that is much better for someone on the path to sports mastery than simply "exercising" but still not quite the same mindset again.

"Working out" is generally considered to be more focused and serious but you can work out all you want, you can work out hard all you want, but you still may or may not have a clearly defined goal or even a plan to reach it. Think of all your own personal experiences when you've been in training; your outlook and focus is a lot different than just exercising or working out.

For the common majority of normal people exercising and working out will be enough but for pro athletes on the path to sports mastery, continuous training is needed. On a related topic, research also shows that history's greatest sports masters alluded to "always" being in training in one way or another. If they were not training their physical body they may have been doing some mental training or watching game footage.

"I would say to myself, forget about tomorrow. What if today were the last day of training you could be remembered for? What if this particular interval that I was doing on the treadmill right now – right now, was the last one I was remembered for? That's how I trained. That's how I approached it." - Apolo Ohno (8-Time U.S. Winter Olympic Medalist)

World Class U.S. Olympic swimmer, Dara Torres, collected five medals at the 2000 Olympics in Sydney, Australia, winning bronze in three individual events and has won 12 Olympic medals over all. At the Beijing Games in 2008, Dara became the oldest swimmer to compete in the Olympics, where she took three silver medals. Her attitude on training is obvious.

How so?

Well, she states, "I swam and did pregnancy-safe lifting exercises 3 to 4 days a week while I was pregnant. I trained up to the <u>day before</u> giving birth." – Dara Torres

Pro tennis star Lindsay Davenport has won three Grand Slam singles tournaments and an Olympic gold medal in singles. In 2008, she also won the Bali Open just three months after having her baby.

At the time of this writing, English long distance runner, Paula Radcliffe, was the current women's world record holder in the marathon with her time of 2:15:25 hours. She is a three-time winner of the London Marathon, two-time New York Marathon champion, and won the 2002 Chicago Marathon. One of her wins in the New York Marathon came less than 10 months after having her baby.

Maximize Your Full Athletic Potential

A crucial part of the sports mastery model is athletic actualization. We have learned that actualization is the highest level you can reach, so this needs to be applied to your physical conditioning as well. Athletic actualization would refer to the highest level of physical fitness and conditioning you can reach. Since, each athlete is different, you have to be consciously aware and focused on actualizing your full athletic potential, not just parts of it.

Whenever you train, you need to be thinking of pushing yourself as far as you safely can…..every time! This type of habit forming training will eventually become "how" you train. The results will show quickly as you surpass others, that are merely doing glorified exercise. When you train you need to be focused and thinking about athletic actualization and how the training session you are in is helping you get closer to reaching it. This in turn will give you extra motivation to train hard as you know you are closing in on your goal.

One of the greatest examples of athletic actualization and how to train, is the late great Jack LaLanne.

"I train like I'm training for the Olympics or for a Mr. America contest, the way I've always trained my whole life." – Jack LaLanne

Recently, many have come to know of Jack LaLanne through television advertisements, but others know him from his amazing feats and athletic achievements. Here are just a few of his spectacular feats:

1954 - Age 40: Swam the length of the San Francisco Golden Gate Bridge underwater with 140 pounds of equipment, including two air tanks… an undisputed world record.

1955 - Age 41: Swam, handcuffed, from Alcatraz to Fisherman's Wharf in San Francisco, CA.

1956 - Age 42: Set a world record of 1,033 pushups in 23 minutes on "You Asked for It", a TV Show with Art Baker.

1957 - Age 43: Swam the treacherous Golden Gate Channel, towing a 2,500-pound cabin cruiser. This involved fighting the cold, swift ocean currents that made the 1 mile swim a 6 ½ mile test of strength and endurance.

1958 - Age 44: Maneuvered a paddle-board 30 miles, 9-½ hours non-stop from Farallon Islands to the San Francisco shore.

1959 - Age 45: Completed 1,000 pushups and 1,000 chin-ups in 1 hour and 22 minutes. (*"The Jack LaLanne Show"* goes nationwide).

1974 - Age 60: Swam from Alcatraz Island to Fisherman's Wharf, for a second time handcuffed, shackled and towing a 1,000-pound boat.

1975 - Age 61: Swam the length of the Golden Gate Bridge, underwater, for a second time handcuffed, shackled and towing a 1,000-pound boat.

1976 - Age 62: Commemorating the "Spirit of '76", swam 1 mile in Long Beach Harbor, handcuffed, shackled and towing 13 boats, (representing the 13 original colonies), containing 76 people.

1979 - Age 65: Towed 65 boats filled with 6,500-pounds of Louisiana Pacific wood pulp while handcuffed and shackled in Lake Ashinoko, near Tokyo, Japan.

1980 - Age 66: Towed 10 boats in North Miami, Florida filled with 77 people for over a mile in less than 1 hour.

1984 - Age 70: Handcuffed, shackled and fighting strong winds and currents, towed 70 boats with 70 people from the Queen's Way Bridge in the Long Beach Harbor to the Queen Mary, 1 ½ miles.

…..Now ask yourself, "Am I doing enough?"

Cross Training: A Hidden Key

Cross training is a very helpful tool for actualizing your full potential. In order to fully actualize your potential, you have to wake up and ignite as much of your physical potential as you can. Now, you don't necessarily have to devote hours and hours to other sports unless you want to, but it's a good idea to get yourself, (mind and body), accustomed to different types of work, movements and experiences in relation to your training. We can think back to many of the greatest athletes in history and though many were known for their excellence in a given sport, many played multiple sports and/or trained in various sports.

Here are a few examples of some greats in sports that obviously benefited from cross training.

Jim Thorpe - *(Track & Field/Football)*

Michael Jordan – *(Basketball/Baseball)*

Lottie Dod - *(Tennis/Field Hockey/Archery/Golf)*

Bo Jackson – *(Baseball/Football - All-Star in Both!)*

Babe Zaharias *(Golf/Tennis/Track & Field)*

Jim Brown – *(Football/Lacrosse)*

Deion Sanders – *(Football/Baseball)*

By training themselves at a high level and in different sports they were able to unlock other facets of their potential. This type of intense cross training, no doubt, helped them reach higher levels in their main sport. Remember, cross training is also great for breaking up your regular routine as it stimulates and uses different muscles, movements, and strategies.

Now, that you have the secret foundation for maximizing your full potential…. Now, you need the nuts and bolts for you to unleash the beast.

Chapter

⑦

The Nuts n' Bolts

To Take You From A

Top Athlete To A Master In Your Sport!

Unleash The Beast

And Make Your

Competition Run For Cover

When You Enter The Arena!

Equipped with a clear understanding of all the preceding levels of the sports mastery model, you also need to understand some of the intangibles that the champions state as being key factors in their success.

Intangibles of Sports Mastery

<u>Deep Understanding of Yourself</u>

A quality found in nearly every champion and sports master….. and one you need to develop is a deep understanding of your own body. In order to reach your maximum levels you must be in constant communication with your body. You must not only know what your own body is capable of, but also what it is telling you.

To do this you have to be really "in tune" with your body. The only person who will truly know when you're tired or if you can "dig deep" and gut out a championship caliber performance …..is you. This in depth knowledge and confidence you get comes from your intense training, experiences and your awareness of them.

This is a very important aspect because when you're in the 2nd overtime of a big game, for example, and everyone else is gasping for air…..you want to "know" that you can dig deep, and take over if needed and win it all.

The more intense training and sports experience you can get, the more you'll come to understand yourself and how you react under certain conditions.

Michael Jordan, regarded as one of the most clutch performers in sports history, stated that he frequently played mental tricks with himself. He would create mental situations during training to simulate various game scenarios.

For instance, after a hard training session, while fatigued, he would pretend in his mind that the clock was winding down and they needed one shot to win. He would create scenarios like these while training so when that situation happened in a real game, his mind and body had already been prepared for it.

So, for Michael Jordan it didn't seem like a clutch shot because he already done it many times before. He knew within himself that he could make the game winning shot while fatigued.

Consistent High Levels of Performance

Sports masters and champions throughout history all had the ability to achieve greatness beyond what was expected of them. They also had the ability to reach a championship level time after time.

"During my routine and even after it, I did not think it was all that perfect. I thought it was pretty good, but athletes don't think about history when making history. They think about what they're doing, and that's how it gets done. Hard work for consistent, excellent results is what matters." – Nadia Comaneci (Gymnast whose unprecedented perfect 10.0 score at the 1976 Montreal Olympics in Montreal has come to exemplify perfection in sports.)

"The difference of great players is at a certain point in a match they raise their level of play and maintain it. Lesser players play great for a set, but then less."
- Pete Sampras (14 Grand Slam Championships)

"Any time you're satisfied with mediocrity, any time you take away incentive from human beings, you've blown it. I'm a perfectionist much more than I'm a super competitor, and there's a big difference there.... I've been painted as a person who only competes.... but most of all, I get off on hitting a shot correctly." –

Billie Jean King (Winner of 12 Grand Slam singles titles, 16 Grand Slam women's doubles titles, and 11 Grand Slam mixed doubles titles.)

Increased time in "the zone"

To the casual onlooker, it may seem that many of the true champions in sports history had the ability to stay "in the zone" for long periods of time which made all their efforts seem easy.

However, once you take a closer look, you'll see that many of the sports masters in history, didn't really consider themselves in the zone much of the time, rather, they felt like this is just "who they were" and "how they played". This is why having a customized plan for sports mastery is crucial because once you reach sports mastery your game play will consistently be at such a high level, that it will seem like you are "always" in the zone.

Anticipation

Anticipation is defined as the ability of looking forward or the visualization of a future event or state. This has always been a very important attribute for any athlete to exhibit. In more recent times, however, this has been referred to as *fast forwarding*.

In sports, this basically refers to the ability to anticipate where the ball, teammates and/or opponents are going to be. We can reference two great athletes for this; **Wayne Gretzky and Cristiano Ronaldo.**

One of the all time legends in professional hockey is Wayne Gretzky and he gives some insight on anticipation. Historically, Gretzky was never very fast, his shot was fairly weak, and he was last in the team in strength training. He would often operate from the small space in the back of the opponent's goal, which he called his "office". He would often anticipate where his team would be well before they got there and feed them passes so unexpectedly he would often surprise them.

*"I skate to where the puck is **going to be**."* - Wayne Gretzky, (Legendary NHL Hall of Famer)

For a cover story in 1985, he told Time Magazine, *"People talk about skating, puck handling and shooting, but the whole sport is angles and caroms; forgetting the straight direction the puck is going, calculating where it will be diverted, factoring in all the interruptions."*

What Wayne Gretzky was describing was the ability to travel forward in time and predict where the puck will emerge and to make his way to the precise spot.

Fast-forwarding in sports involves the ability to anticipate the flow of play and stay ahead of the game in real time. Athletes who fast-forward anticipate where teammates and the competition are going to be. Using this technique provides a huge competitive advantage and also makes other teammates perform better.

Fast-forwarding is about anticipation, being steps ahead of others in thinking visioning, and predicting outcomes from one's experience as quickly as possible. Having talent, strength and speed are great but, an intangible quality, like fast forwarding is also needed to anticipate effectively.

Another athlete with strong fast-forwarding skills is Portuguese soccer player, Cristiano Ronaldo. Ronaldo scored 42 goals during the 2007 season for Manchester United and led his team to the English Premier League and UEFA Champions League titles. He also earned both player-of-the-year awards for the second year in a row.

"The guy has tremendous field awareness, a great feel for the game. I can compare it to chess players, who are three or four moves ahead of everybody else." - Thomas Rongen (Coach of the under-20 USA soccer team speaking of Cristiano Ronaldo)

Knowing What to Do

In the area of sports mastery, this has been coined as *situational sports intelligence*. This comes from a deep understanding of yourself, your sport, the situation you or your team is currently in, and what needs to be done in order to achieve the desired results.....which is to win.

"Every player competes at a certain level, but there are special players who really are able to intuitively understand situations that help win games, whether it's a steal, an offense board at the appropriate time, having the fortitude to shoot the 3 when maybe it's not exactly called for." – Gregg Poppovich, (Head Coach of 4 Time NBA Championship San Antonio Spurs)

Synergy

No matter what sport you are involved in or how much training you have done previously, none of that will matter much if the parts are not working together. In sports mastery, this is referred to as synergy but in layman terms can be called *"putting it together"*.

Mark Twain even referred to synergy as "the bonus that is achieved when things work together harmoniously".

"The compound workout she is driven through is designed to teach her muscles to be stronger together – not stronger apart. The finely tuned neuromuscular network she constantly builds upon means her body works together in all the right places." – Dara Torres (Winner of 12 Olympic Medals)

"Synergy is the highest activity of life; it creates new untapped alternatives; it values and exploits the mental, emotional, and psychological differences between people." – Stephen Covey (Best-selling author and educator)

Many athletes, train hard, practice hard and do what their coaches tell them, but for some reason they just can't seem to put it together. This is becoming an increasing problem even with top pro athletes today. Possibly one of the most important aspects in your progression toward sports mastery is the synergy or the ability to "put it all together".

You need to be able to incorporate experiences from your sport and game play with your physical body fully actualized along with your expert knowledge, intelligence and ethics. These all need to work together in harmony in order to reach sports mastery. Once all these levels have been reached and are synergistically working together in unison, you will be able reach your highest levels and master your sport.

When you reach sports mastery, you will be able to win consistently, silence the critics and gain respect from your coaches and peers. Not only that, but you will gain the kind of respect that even money can't buy……self-respect.

Chapter

R-E-S-P-E-C-T,

Just A Little Bit –

Feels Pretty Good

To Be A

Winner, Huh?

Have you ever thought of what sports are really all about and why we even play them in the first place? The textbook definition of *sport* is *"an activity involving physical exertion and skill that is governed by a set of rules or customs and often undertaken competitively or as recreation."* Human civilization has been involved in sports as far back as the gladiator fights and ancient Olympics.

An example of the more recent forms are the NBA, MLB, and the NFL. Competitive sports have a tremendous impact on our culture. It influences the values of millions of participants and spectators. This is what's so important for the aspiring sports master to understand.

If we go back in history, we see that sports have invoked a great deal of public interest. However, unlike the days of old, results are no longer decided by the king or an emperor. Now, we have referees, umpires, and judges that applies **rules and regulations** to every sport.

It's these rules and regulations that spark debates on ethics, sportsmanship and gamesmanship. For sports masters, this is another level that sets them apart from the rest.

Although, there are many examples of good sportsmanship, unethical sports-related behavior does occur.

Even top super-star athletes nowadays, will sometimes do "whatever it takes" to win a game…..or to "bend the rules" a bit to give him or herself an advantage. These types of antics have no place in the expression of a sports master. Cheating and misconduct, (even among the spectators), by using commercialization and professional connections are just a few of the tactics used to provide an unethical and competitive advantage.

We see many of these disruptive actions occur during game play and many apply specifically to its own sport.

No doubt, we've all heard terms like…. being a "good sport", "having good sportsmanship" or displaying "unsportsmanlike conduct".

Although, these terms are usually thrown around loosely, the sports masters and true champions use these principles as a guide and reference for "playing the right way"; not only that, but winning the right way as well.

Sportsmanship

From a sports master or true champion's point of view, the way he/she plays the game is key. One of the great aspects of sports is that it is one of the rare activities where you can gain, *or* lose honor. The sports master's ideal goal would be to engage in honorable competition while pursuing victory.

The sports masters follow what they call their "Master Code" and this ethical and moral stage of the sports mastery model demands a commitment to principles, integrity and honor. This includes abiding by and playing within the confines of the rules and regulations associated with the sport.

Recently, we've seen top super-star athletes try and "get away" with bending or breaking some of the rules of the game. Sports masters don't try to "cheat" the system or "fool the ref" or get away with sneaky tricks to gain an edge, even if they could.

One of the reasons why integrity and honor have gone away from pro sports today is because many coaches and players who practice good sportsmanship are often at a disadvantage when competing against others who will do anything to win, including cheating and breaking rules. For this reason, even many "good sports" often follow suit and imitate some of these dishonorable practices in an attempt to, at least, even the playing field.

A true champion is willing to lose the game rather than sacrifice ethical principles to win. It may seem tough to swallow, but winning through dishonesty rarely ever proves to have a positive outcome. In fact, most times, winning by *"dishonorable means"* has a counter effect reflecting negatively on the athlete, team or organization.

A victory attained by cheating or other forms of unethical conduct is not only dishonorable but unearned. A sports master believes that winning without honor is not a true victory. Trainers and coaches would do well to remind themselves and their athletes that true competition means not only the pursuit of the win, but pursuing victory with honor. If you aren't willing to lose, you may be willing to do unethical things to win.

It would be wise to remember the old saying, *"Success without honor is an unseasoned dish; it will satisfy your hunger, but it won't taste good."*

Gamesmanship

Most times, we hear the terms unsportsmanlike conduct, unethical, dishonorable game play, cheating, etc., but all these can be grouped under the more recent term….. *Gamesmanship*. Gamesmanship refers to ways of bending, evading and breaking the rules to provide a competitive advantage.

The following are some examples of the gamesmanship mentality and some tactics that are often used in order to gain a competitive advantage. Phrases and thoughts like:

"It's the officials' job to catch me"

"It ain't cheatin'…. unless you get caught."

"It's the officials' job to enforce the rules and not our responsibility to follow them.

Examples of gamesmanship tactics in sports

Faked Fouls – Belief that it is acceptable to fake fouls.

Illegal Head Start – Belief that it is acceptable to get an illegal head start in cross country track or leaving the line early in soccer to block a penalty kick.

Doctoring Equipment – Belief that it is acceptable to illegally "doctor" a baseball or a bat. How about raising the foul line slightly to keep bunts in play to favor a home team or altering the height of the mound or distance from the rubber to the plate?

Sneaky (underhanded) Personal Fouls – Belief it is acceptable in soccer, water polo, basketball and football to illegally hold, grab and pull on opponents.

Taking a Player Out – Belief that injuring an opponent or aggravating his/her pre-existing injury to take the opponent out of the game is legitimate.

We've seen more and more frequently coaches who gain an advantage by violating eligibility, recruiting and practice rules just as gamesmanship athletes gain an advantage by using illegal performance-enhancing drugs and dishonorable playing tactics.

Sportsmanship promotes safety and the integrity of the game, while gamesmanship promotes tactics and practices that may be unsafe and can violate the integrity of the game.

Some examples include, throwing at a batter for any reason, physical intimidation, intentional injuring, tripping and similar tactics, often justified as "part of the game", introduces dangerous elements into the game. **Rules** establish standards of fair play and define the game. Violating the rules and regulations can endanger the sport and the athletes themselves.

Integrity of the Sport

Every sport has developed over the years with rule refinements to maintain integrity. When behavior patterns develop that corrupt the game, such as **chop blocking** or **spear tackling** in football, **flagrant fouls** or **undercutting** in basketball…. the matters are addressed by additional rules or instructions to officials to enforce existing rules.

Gamesmanship tactics that change the nature of the game are unethical because they violate the integrity of the sport. Here are some examples to help you see the difference.

Intentional Strategic Fouls

In some sports, specific penalties are prescribed for specific rule violations, such as delay of game and personal fouls in basketball. In these specific situations, the traditions of the sports permit a player to "take the penalty" by deliberately violating the rule for strategic reasons. Coaches teach players when and how to make the decision to intentionally foul as a strategy of the game.

Undetected Fouls

If, <u>intentional rule violations,</u> like pulling shirts in soccer or tripping in hockey are a legitimate part of the game, the skill of fouling and avoiding detection is important and should be taught by coaches like any other legitimate technique. This places great value on non-athletic skills.

Taunting

Most *taunting* is amateurish and ineffective. If taunting and "trash talking" are a legitimate part of the game to unsettle an opponent or pump oneself up, why don't we <u>teach</u> athletes to do it? Why not teach athletes to refer to hurtful, private information about an opponent? Why not have psychologists train athletes to really get under someone's skin? After all, anything worth doing…. is worth doing well! As absurd as that sounds, many athletes have been guilty of using taunting as a tactic.

Equipment Tampering

The clearest example of unethical tactics is *equipment tampering*. Illegally altering equipment to gain an advantage violates the integrity of the sport and can also be dangerous to the players. Illegal alteration of the playing field is also corruption of the sport.

Cheating

Cheating is defined as: Deliberately violating the rules or traditions of a game to gain an unfair advantage.

In some sports, like basketball and hockey, established traditions of the game permit a player to foul an opponent and take a penalty as a matter of strategy. This is not cheating.

Faking Injuries

It is not honest or trustworthy to fake an injury to gain advantage or extra time. It is not honest or trustworthy to fool an official into making a bad call.

Many volleyball coaches train their players to call a "touch" if a ball hit s them before going out of bounds and the official missed the play.

In tennis, many coaches consider it proper sportsmanship to call a ball out that the umpire did not call.

Golfers are expected to report extra strokes and call penalties on themselves.

Sports Masters and true champions alike practice showing respect to athletes, officials and fans. They even show respect for their opponents.

Win or Lose With Class

Bragging or boasting of victory are forms of unsportsmanlike behavior, as are complaining, blaming bad luck on officials and whining in defeat. Celebrations that demean an opponent or appear overly self-congratulatory are unsportsmanlike.

There's an old saying; *"An athlete who scores ought to act as if he/she has done it before."* When engaged in coaching, coaches must recognize the power they hold over athletes and therefore make reasonable efforts to avoid engaging in conduct that is personally demeaning to athletes and other participants.

Accountability

One of the most overlooked qualities of a sports master is *accountability.* True champions and sports masters both hold themselves accountable most times when their team loses a game or when a play doesn't run correctly, even if when it's not their fault. They rarely blame anyone else if they lose or something doesn't go as plan. Research shows that many of the greats in sports often held themselves responsible because they felt like they should have been able to do something to change the outcome for the better.

Once you have reached your goal of sports mastery you will gain the respect of others and yourself. You will be seen as a true champion, not a phony who cheated his/her way to the championship or got there through dishonorable means. There is no better feeling than knowing you've reached your highest levels through work, dedication and honor……..competed against the best and came out victorious.

Fans, critics, and skeptics will have no choice, but to be silent or convert to your supporter. When you reach your highest levels of performance and do it the "right way", with integrity and honor, you will be well on your way to cementing a legacy that will etch your name into the sports history books.

Chapter

How To Win

Multiple Championships

And

Cement A Legacy

That Will

Etch Your Name Into

Sports History

As A True Champion

When you reach your highest levels of performance and do it the "right way"....with integrity and honor, you will be well on your way to cementing a legacy that will etch your name into the sports history books.

Now that you have a clear understanding of all the preceding levels of the sports mastery model and you've been putting it together, now the only thing you need is an expert to guide you on the path to mastery. If you've won a championship or two or three, but have recently "lost it", you may want to consider enlisting the services of a sports mastery artisan. When obstacles occur, a qualified opinion that takes into account the overall goal of sports mastery that is specific to <u>you</u> will save you many months of time and wasted energy. Time and efficiency is of prime importance.

In relation to the aforementioned sports mastery model, here is what's called "The Five Sheaths" of sports mastery. Once all the levels of the sports mastery model have been reached, these attributes are synergistically layered within the athlete. This is an illustration of the protective layers, called sheaths that intertwine, protect, and guide the sports master. (See Fig. 1-c).

Fig. 1-c.

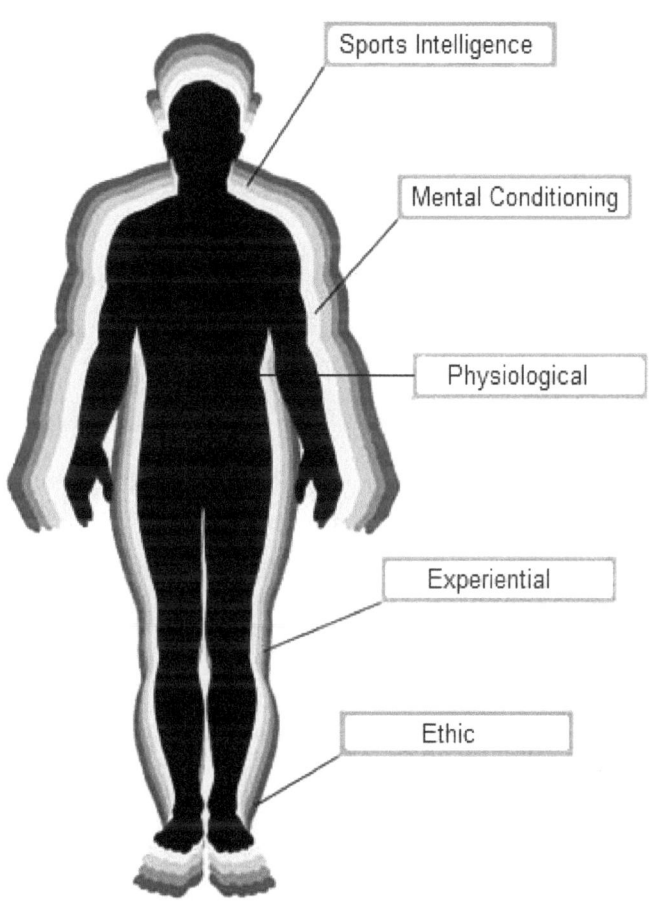

Eight Instances When You Need Sports Mastery

1). When you think your coach doesn't know how to win

2). When you think you can't relate to your players anymore

3). When you are sick and tired of losing

4). When you are tired of everybody "bad mouthing" you and your team

5). When you are constantly the butt of derogatory jokes regarding your game performance

6). When half of your nicknames are negative in nature

7). When you feel like you need a fresh, new outlook and specific plan of action custom for you and your team

8). When you've tried everything and don't know what else to do

Sports Mastery for Coaches and Trainers

Sports mastery also applies to coaches and trainers as well. Both coaches and trainers, need to begin to apply mastery techniques to their philosophy and training regimens with their athletes as soon as possible.

Many of the past coaches who have led teams to multiple championships have all embraced these same principles. You may not have thought about it before, but it can be said that these types of dynasty-building coaches were, no doubt, masters at coaching in their sport. Think about all the coaches in any sport that have consistently won big, and you'll see an obvious commonality. They may have said it slightly different but, we can see that the same principles are present and practiced.

"Winning is not a sometime thing.....it's an all the time thing. You don't win once in a while...... you don't do things right once in a while..... you do them right all of the time. Winning is a habit. Unfortunately, so is losing." -Vince Lombardi, (5-Time NFL Championship Winner, Coach of the Year '59)

"***Success*** *is peace of mind which is a direct result of self-satisfaction in knowing you made the effort to become the best of which you are capable.*" – John Wooden, (10 NCAA Men's Basketball Championships)

"***Excellence*** *is the gradual result of always striving to do better.*"- Pat Riley, (7 NBA Championship Titles)

"*The strength of the team is each individual member...the strength of each member is the team.*"- Phil Jackson, (13 NBA Championship Titles)

For coaches that want the best for their teams, sports mastery is the ideal choice. Coaches should be able to ask their sports mastery artisan suggestions and advice on implementing a custom philosophy in line with their own personal system, but not limited to developing a completely new strategy if needed. Remember, for coaches, trainers and athletes alike, sports mastery is a ongoing mission and you will continually be redefining and improving your own style of mastery.

This is actually the fun part, because as you continually unlock more of your potential (or, if you're a coach or trainer….. your team's potential), it is a very gratifying and rewarding feeling.

Coaches that consistently lead their teams to championships all pay great attention to detail with a focus on excellence, a focus on sports mastery. Once you do this, winning is merely a side benefit and you can win pretty much at will, until you meet another sports master, which you will obviously relish. This leads us to another often overlooked attribute of a sports master.

Since sports masters have ascended the standard levels of professional competition, they always welcome the opportunity to engage in some good wholesome highly advanced competition. At some point, especially as you start your progression, you will see that you are becoming so far ahead of the game that you may find yourself somewhat bored and will also be looking forward to some good competition.

Although rare, (because most never make it to a level to even win enough to become bored), if this does set in, a sports master will, no doubt, find more and more ways to continually improve his/her style of sports mastery.

Looking into the world of martial arts, the masters even attest to the fact that once they became "masters", it became evident just how little they actually knew. This lending itself to the fact that mastery would be an ongoing process…. one that is constantly progressing and evolving. This is another important aspect to etch your name into the sports history books. One thing to never underestimate is the value and power of your continual evolution. Simply put, we should always strive to learn more and grow in a physical, mental and spiritual way. We are never to old to learn or try new principles and technologies especially when it will greatly benefit your overall goals.

If you win multiple championships or events, depending on your sport, and do this in an honorable way while exhibiting integrity, this is indeed rare and you will, no doubt, be remembered with your legacy cemented. The way to keep winning championships is to get on the path to sports mastery.

It should be clear; if you are not getting the results you want there are only 2 things you need to do.

You need to:

1). Stop what you're doing, think about _why_ you're doing what you're doing and if it's actually helping you achieve your goal.

2). Take the quick customized assessment to see if you're really ready to win big and master your sport at *Psionova.com* - Get your results, then contact a sports mastery artisan and get on the path to sports mastery.

To Your Mastery,

J. Scott Warner

Psionova Research & Development

About the Author

J. Scott Warner is the founder of Psionova, a leading research and actualization company. He has been at the forefront of cutting edge performance, sports mastery and athletic actualization for years now. Ensuring top athletes all over the world get on the path to sports mastery, J. Scott Warner guides pro athletes, coaches and trainers using their own customized blueprint for success.

J. Scott has been called the "schoolmaster" by athletes, coaches and other artisans with his revolutionary system which gives insight on how to win multiple championships. His concepts, philosophies and trainings have been directly responsible for the success of many athletes, coaches and trainers today.

Growing up as a child, J. Scott had already began his own personal quest for sports mastery; finding ways to achieve the highest levels of human potential and athletic performance.

J. Scott is a dedicated athlete himself and has been his entire life. His spark and passion for winning and actualization, however, seems to have been triggered from what he calls "one of the toughest losses" in his life."

What loss was *this*?

It was losing in a championship Junior High School game, in front of the entire school. The embarrassment and humiliation he felt was so intense and hurtful that he devoted himself to figuring out ways to make sure he never had to endure that type of pain ever again. By the early age of 13 years old, J. Scott was unknowingly cultivating his own system for maximizing athletic potential; a system for **athletic mastery.** Back then, he would use a big, old, dusty VHS video recorder to video tape his own backyard games, races, and even training sessions.

He would then go home and go over the tapes for hours and hours looking for holes, gaps, and areas for improvement in his own personal athletic development. He has won many awards and trophies in baseball and track as a youngster.

He continually played, practiced, watched, studied and trained to the max in a variety of sports, including martial arts.

It didn't take long for J. Scott to realize that the greatest sports figures in history had left behind clues for us to follow. He researched and modeled himself after hundreds of top athletes and champions of recent history and compiled decades worth of useful data to be implemented.

At the university, he studied rigorously and immediately took a great liking to psychology, philosophy, physics and chemistry. He immediately began applying principles to his own development and shortly thereafter, made the college basketball team.

From there, he went on to play with and against pro basketball players, pro tournaments, traveling teams and semi-pro teams. During off seasons, he would train athletes getting ready for college and pro tryouts on maximizing their full potential and developing a system specifically for each one.

Every team, men and women, that J. Scott has coached or consulted with, has made it to their championship game, with many winning it all. Not to mention, J. Scott and his own personal teams collected an impressive number of championships themselves.

J. Scott teaches top athletes specific attitudes, skills and knowledge not taught in any university or professional training organization using the power of *Sports Mastery* and *The Athletic Mastery and Sports Synergy System* ™.

If you are ready to challenge your assumptions about the steps you must take to get yourself on the path to sports mastery and win multiple championships in the new millennium, you'll be glad that you met J. Scott Warner. Your personal and professional success has never been closer at hand until this book; *"The Strangest Secret to Winning Championships: How to Crush Your Competition and Totally Dominate Your Sport"*.

www.ingramcontent.com/pod-product-compliance
Lightning Source LLC
Chambersburg PA
CBHW042321150426
43192CB00001B/8